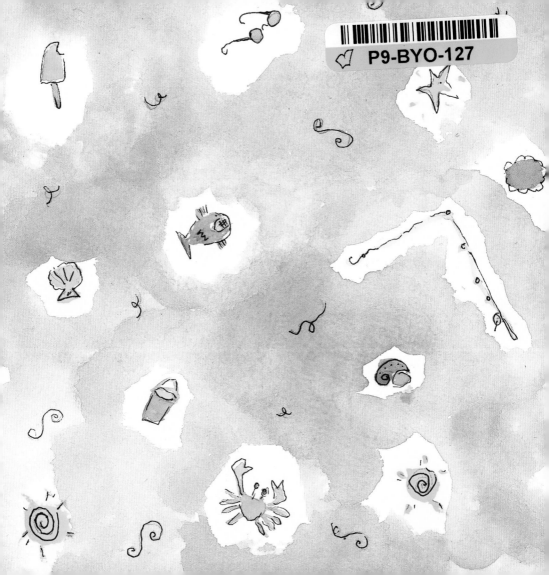

Laura,

Life at the beach wouldn't be the same without you. You are very special and my heart feels very warm when I am in your company. Merry Xmas 2004 — MUYGEN

Love
Dale

Xmas 2003

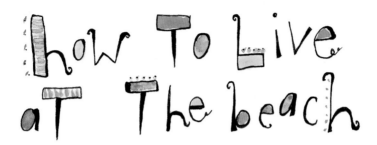

how To Live aT The beach

by
sandy gingras

DOWN
THE
SHORE
PUBLISHING

Down The Shore Publishing Corp.
Box 3100, Harvey Cedars, NJ 08008
www.down-the-shore.com

The words "Down The Shore" and the Down The Shore Publishing logo
are a registered U.S. Trademark.

Printed in China.
10 9 8 7 6 5 4 3 2
Second Printing 2001, with author's revisions

Library of Congress Cataloging-in-Publication Data
Gingras, Sandy, 1958-
    How to live at the beach / by Sandy Gingras.
      p. cm.
    "A Cormorant book."
    ISBN 0-945582-73-0 (cloth)
    1. Conduct of life. 2. Beaches--Miscellanea. I. Title.

BJ1595 .G46 2001
  170'.44--dc21

                              00-065870

In memory of
my mother and father

who brought me to a
little pink house at the beach
and taught me about thankfulness.

how To Live aT The beach

At the beach, life is different. A day moves not from hour to hour but leaps from mood to moment. We go with the currents, plan around the tides, follow the sun.

We measure happiness by nothing we can hold...

...nothing

we can catch.

Everywhere...

PLOP!

Life is jumping and elusive

and
momentously
momentary

We want to elongate the days, distill the memories, make them last. At the same time, we know that the beauty is in the evanescence... Every wave comes in, then retreats. Every day promises, then turns its back and slips away. Every joy has a little tease in it, a give and a take, and leaves

the perfect wave

So we do the best thing
we can do... open up The

windows To our senses

(so we can hear The waves
wwwiiiiissshhhing
inTo The nighT)

and LeT our hearTs Lead us
back To...

The Land of Simplicity

Of minnows and sno-cones and

how the wind blows

flip-flops and hammocks

and don't look at the clocks

crack the crabs a roll in the sand

preserve the wetlands

corn-on-the-cob the fish that robbed

forget about the job

porch swings and daydreams mmm...

sleepy pies

and moonbeams...

And if we allow these moments
To stick to us like sand...

our lives can become castles.

At the beach, treasure is what we find
I hope it's alive
I hope it smells and I can roll in it...
yikes...
not what we buy.

The beach is where we remember

how to shine,

how to peel ourselves down to essence

and shed our shells,

how To reduce

speed.

Simplicity is an unbuttoning of what we've learned to wear as a self -- a looser fit, a softer fabric. It's like a step we've forgotten how to dance, a native language we've forgotten how to speak in a rushy complex world.

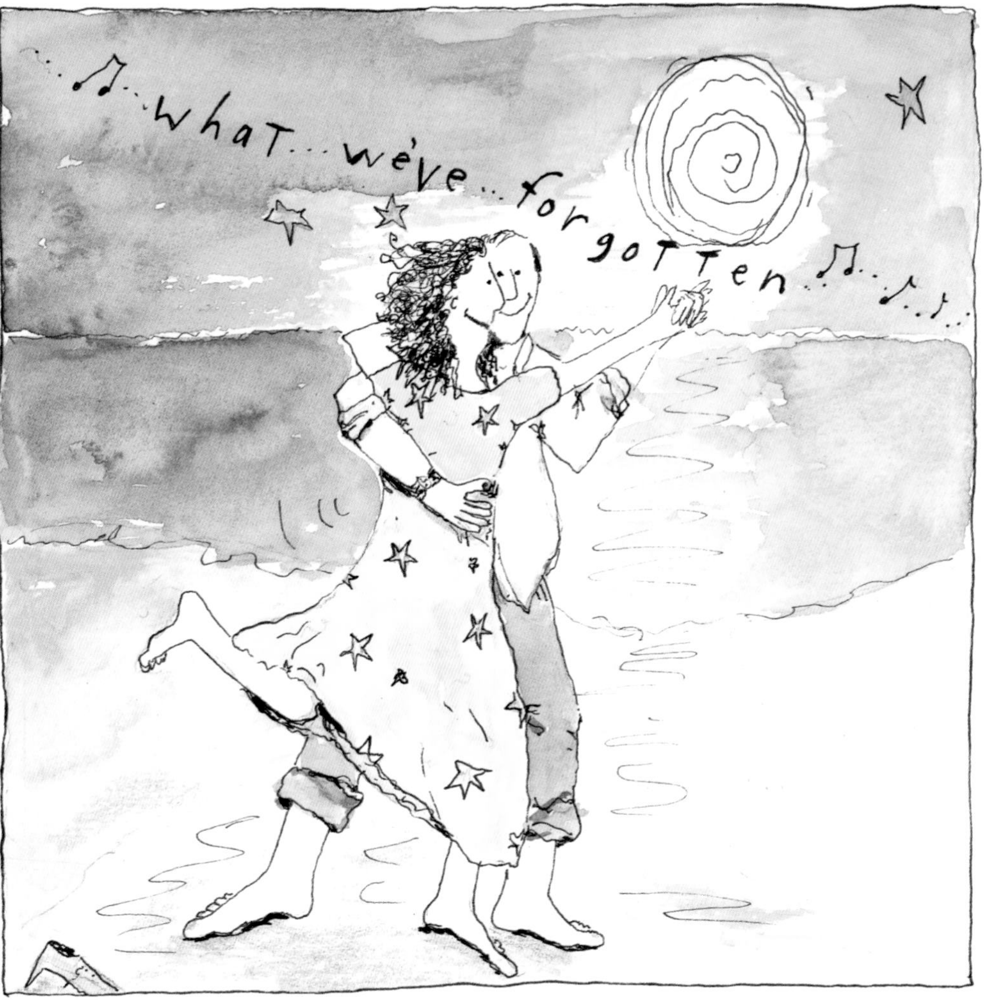
...what...we've...forgotten...

We know that simplicity is within us and within

our grasp.

BUT SiMpLiCiTY is noT SiMpLe
To geT To someTimes...

MosT peopLe have forgoTTen how
To geT away from iT aLL.

Some people are so focused on other things that they miss

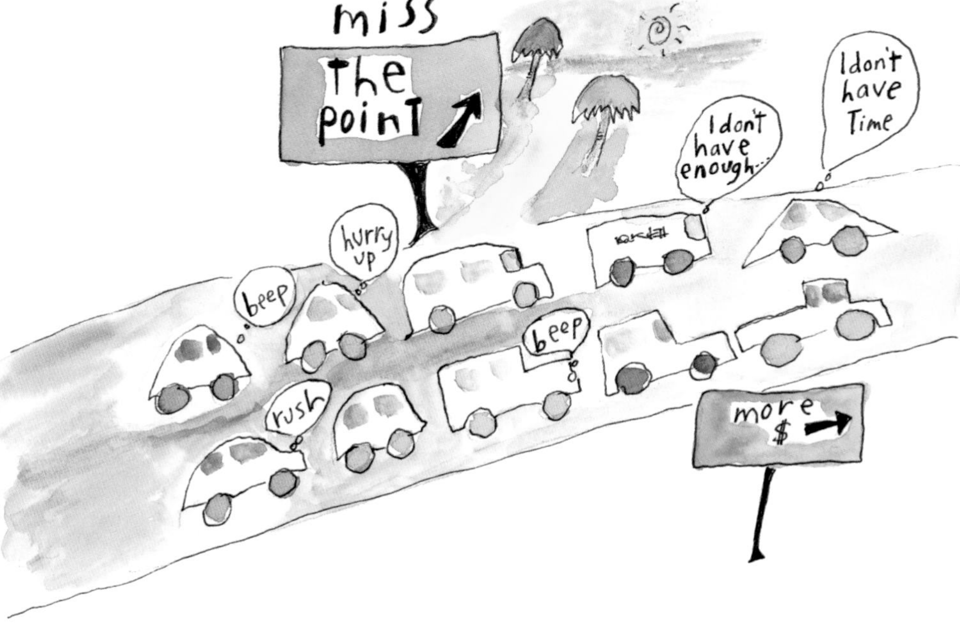

Some people believe that simplicity is something that they can buy.
The beach house
U.S.S. Simplicity

Yet, no matter who comes to the beach, and no matter how lofty the castle they build, Time and tide and wind (and other mysterious forces) will eventually get to them...

and change them...
and maybe even flatten them...

Thankfully

People keep coming back
to the beach (and, for that matter
to love) for this lesson:
Sometimes it's best to
get your walls knocked over
and lose your most
cherished constructs
and be fully
swept
away.

Simplicity is a process.

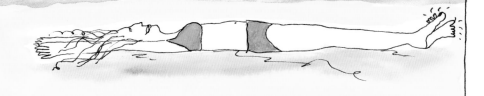

It's a kind of surrender.

It's a forgetting
of the rules we never liked
much anyway, **shoes required**

of the values that have no real value,

accumulation
stuff | **more stuff** | **The schedule** | **the look**

of the goals that never
made much sense anyway.

miserable until I retire road...

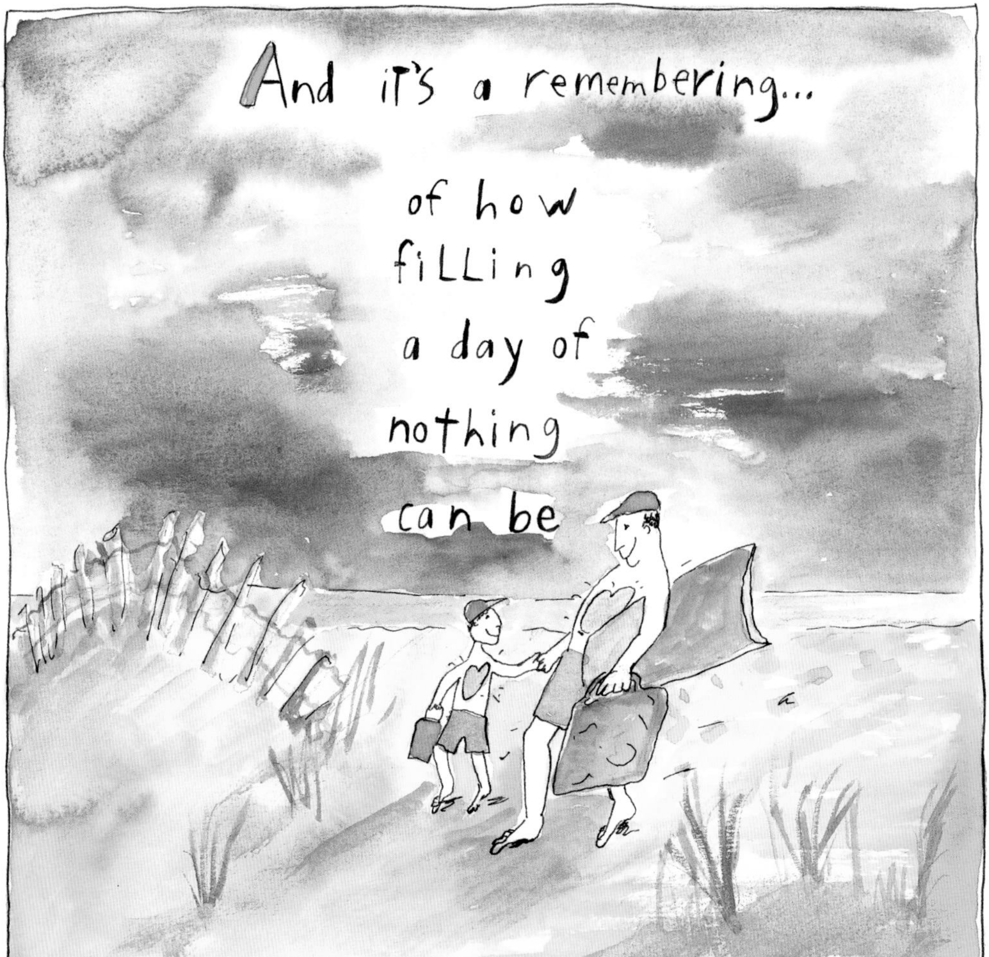
And it's a remembering...
of how
filling
a day of
nothing
can be

how easy it is

To be upLifTed

And so, LiTTLe miracles appear in every crack in the schedule where the unexpected is allowed and the moment gets watered with attention.

the moment

The beach returns us
to our childlike selves, frees us
to be our most elemental, most
beach-bummy-easy selves.

20% water
20% laziness
20% sunshine
20% disorder
18% body fat
1% worthwhile thought
1% bathing suit

We let sandy feet in

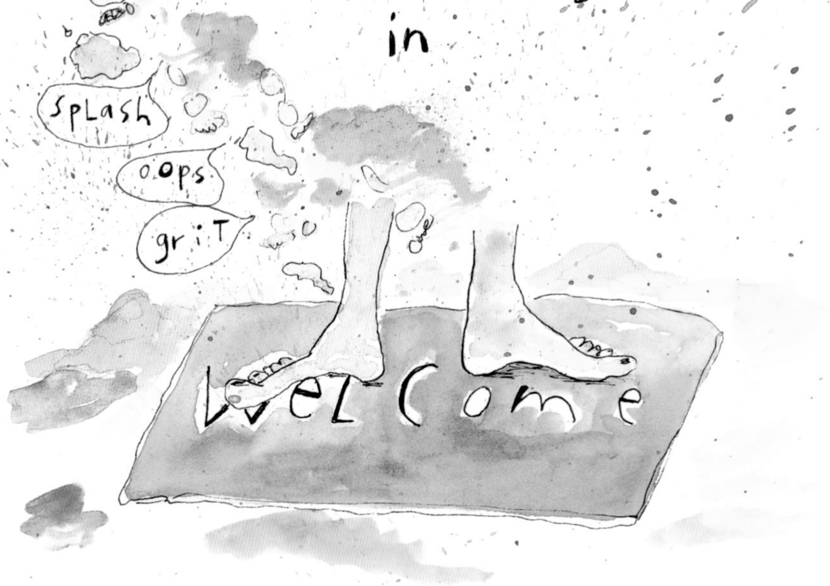

We plan on a LiTTLe rusT.
hon, is This aLL that's LefT of my bicycLe from Last year?
is this our fence? where did the fence go?

The beach is where
there's no such thing
as overgrown.

Where floundering

is natural

and superficial

can be super

Where sometimes it feels just right to be

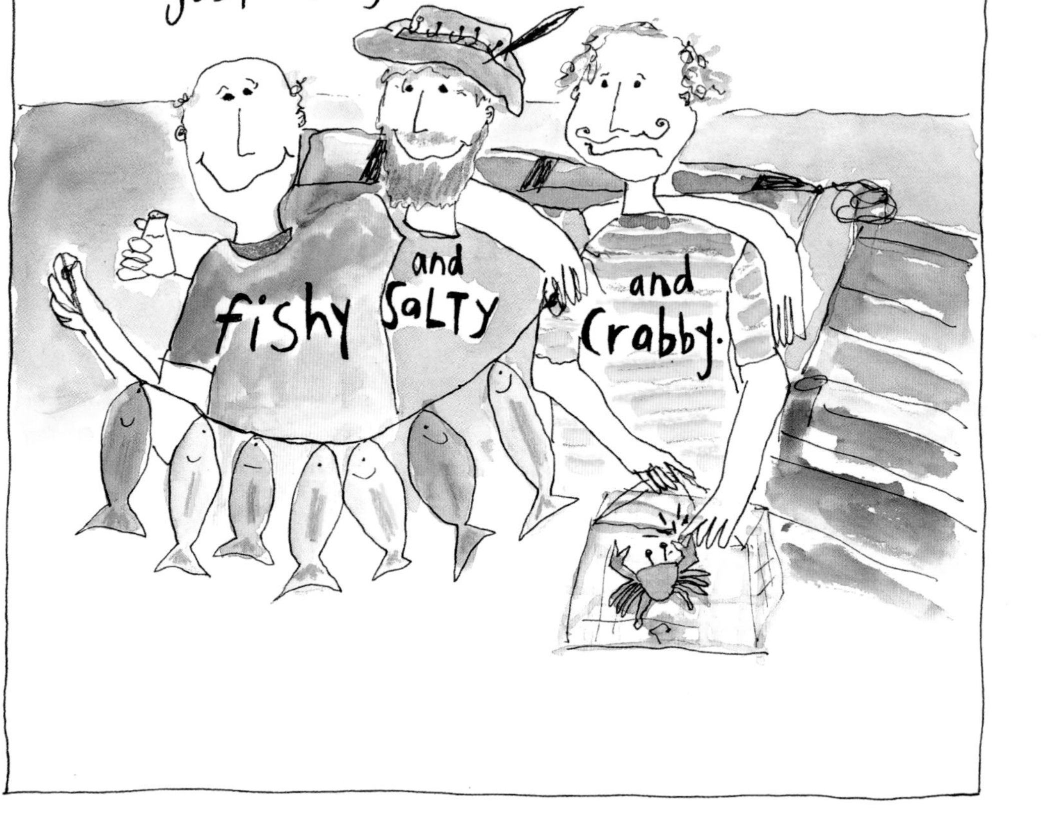

The beach is not as much about slackness of mind (although there is some good in that) as it is about mindfulness to small and simple things.

The beach Teaches us

to redefine rush

It sinks us

into contentment

and keeps building
us up

where we act

a LiTTLe fishy

and casting into the skies.

where we become

star fishermen

IT molds us into the shape

of Thankfulness

We keep getting the chance to transform ourselves. With any shift of wind or weight, we know we can come about...

and we can keep on coming about.

And that slow, crooked
seemingly aimless
path of our
Lives at
The beach

may just be
us getting
closer
and closer
To our best selves.

The end

About the Author

Sandy Gingras is an artist and writer with her own design company called "How To Live". (visit her website at www.how-to-live.com) She and her son, three cats and a fat yellow Labrador live next to a salt marsh on Long Beach Island, New Jersey, where she is active in efforts to preserve open space and wetlands.

———————————

If you liked this book, you may also enjoy
How To Live on an Island
by Sandy Gingras
ISBN 0-945582-57-9 $11.95   hardcover

"...there's no truer place than an island."

———————————

Down The Shore Publishing offers other book and calendar titles (with a special emphasis on the mid-Atlantic coast). For a free catalog, or to be added to our mailing list, just send us a request:

Down The Shore Publishing
P.O. Box 3100
Harvey Cedars, NJ 08008

www.down-the-shore.com